# Best of Friends

Designed By
## Roni Akmon

Edited By
## Nancy Akmon

Blushing Rose Publishing
San Anselmo, California

*Little deeds of kindness,*
*Little words of love,*
*Help to make earth happy*
*like the heaven above.*

*Julia A. F. Carney*
*"Little Things"*

She gained from heaven,
(twas all she wished)
a friend.

Thomas Gray

FRANCIS C JONES 1886

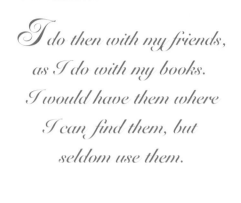

*I do then with my friends,*
*as I do with my books.*
*I would have them where*
*I can find them, but*
*seldom use them.*

Ralph Waldo Emerson

*Flattery makes friends
and truth makes enemies.*

Proverb

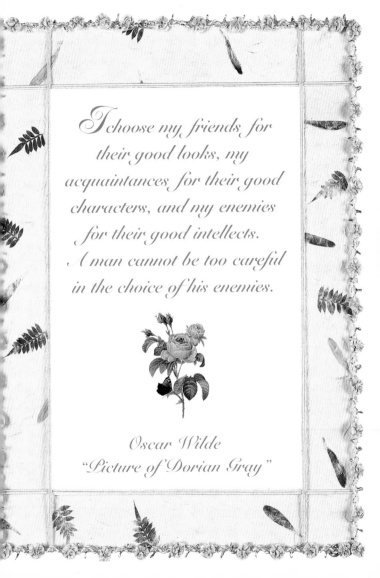

*I choose my friends for their good looks, my acquaintances for their good characters, and my enemies for their good intellects. A man cannot be too careful in the choice of his enemies.*

Oscar Wilde
"Picture of Dorian Gray"

*Fate chooses our relatives, we choose our friends.*

*Jacques Delille*

A Summer Shower.

*Friends should consider themselves as the sacred guardians of each other's virtue; and the noblest testimony they can give of their affection is the correction of the faults of those they love.*

*Anna Letitia Barbauld*
*"On Friendship"*

*False friends are waur
than bitter enemies.*

Scottish Proverb

*Bless me in this life with but peace of my conscience, command of my affections, the love of Thyself and my dearest friends, and I shall be happy enough to pity Caesar.*

Sir Thomas Browne
"Religio Medici"

*Books and friends*
*should be few but good.*

Proverb

The proper office of a friend is to side with you when you are wrong. Nearly anybody will side with you when you are right.

Mark Twain

Be the same to your
friends, whether in
prosperity or adversity.

Periander

There are companions
to keep one company,
And there is a friend more
devoted than a brother.

Old Testament
"Proverbs 18.24"

Be friends with the
friendly, and visit
him who visits you.

Hesiod

*Oil and incense gladden the heart,- And the sweetness of a friend is better than one's own counsel. Do not desert your friend and your father's friend; -Do not enter your brother's house in your time of misfortune;- A close neighbor is better than a distant brother.*

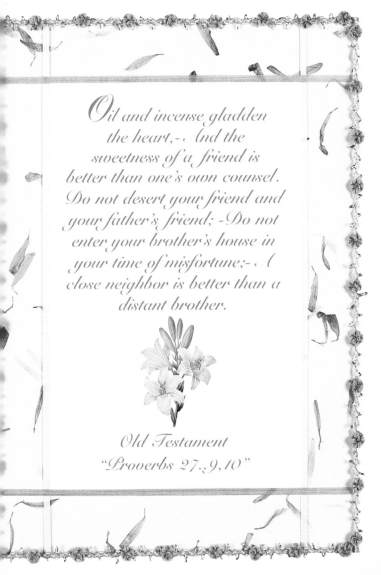

*Old Testament*
*"Proverbs 27.:9,10"*

*At need shall men prove their friends.*

Robert Mannyng

*As old wood is best to burn, old horse to ride, old books to read, and old wine to drink, so are friends always most trusty to use.*

*Leonard Wright*
*"Display of Dutie"*

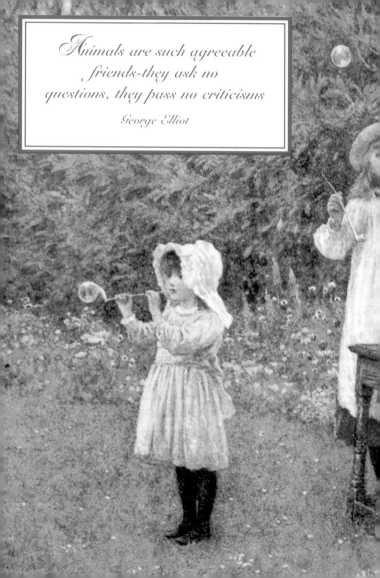

*Animals are such agreeable friends-they ask no questions, they pass no criticisms*

*George Elliot*

Are new friends who are worthy of friendship, to be preferred to old friends?... -as in the case of wines that improve with age, the oldest friendships ought to be the most delightful; moreover, the old adage is true: "Men must eat many a peck of salt together before the claims of friendship are fulfilled."

Marcus Tullius Cicero
"De Amicitia"

There are two elements that go into friendship, each so sovereign that I can detect no superiority in either,....-One is Truth. A friend is a person with whom I may be sincere. Before him I may think aloud....-The other element of friendship is Tenderness....-When a man becomes dear to me I have touched the goal of fortune....-I wish friendship should have feet, as well as eyes and eloquence. It must plant itself on the ground before it walks over the moon... -The essence of friendship is entireness, a total magnanimity and trust. It must not surmise or provide for infirmity. It treats its object as a god, that it may defy both.

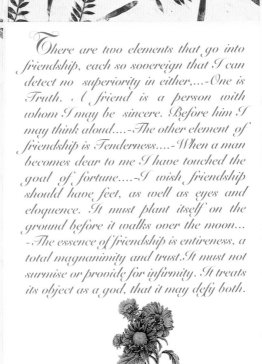

Ralph Waldo Emerson
"Friendship and Love"

Designed by Roni Akmon

Certain illustrations in this book are reprinted with
permission of: Fine Art Photographic Library,
Bridgeman Art Library and Mary Evans Picture Library.
Cover:"Best Friends", by Hans Anderson Brenckilde
1998 Artists Rights Society, NY/Copy-Dan, Copenhagen
"Poppies c. 1909 by Frederick Stead (1863-1940) Bradford
Art Galleries & Museums/Bridgeman Art Library London.

Efforts have been made to find the copyright holders
of material used in this publication. We apologize for
any omissions or errors and will be pleased to include
the appropriate acknowledgements in fiutre editions.

ISBN# 1-884807-27-5

Blushing Rose Publishing
P.O. Box 2238
San Anselmo, Ca. 94979
www.blushingrose.com

Printed and bound in China